T0303789

BRITISH INDUSTRIAL RAILWAYS 1960s–1980s

JOHN GLOVER

AMBERLEY

First published 2023

Amberley Publishing
The Hill, Stroud
Gloucestershire, GL5 4EP

www.amberley-books.com

Copyright © John Glover, 2023

The right of John Glover to be identified as
the Author of this work has been asserted in
accordance with the Copyrights, Designs and
Patents Act 1988.

ISBN 978 1 3981 1194 3 (print)
ISBN 978 1 3981 1195 0 (ebook)

British Library Cataloguing in Publication Data.
A catalogue record for this book is available from
the British Library.

Origination by Amberley Publishing.
Printed in the UK.

Introduction

Industrial railways were conceived as a number of individual developments to meet the needs of the industries that created them. They were for local purposes, sometimes within the works site only. Here, there was no need to comply with the regulations for movements on the national railway. But industrial railways were also used as feeders to waterways and later to exchange sidings with what became the main line railway system. In the early years they might have had different technical characteristics, maybe with track of different gauges, and perhaps used untried or even experimental technology. In nearly all cases they were for the carriage of goods, not passengers.

The developing main line railways were concerned with the movement of aggregates, agricultural goods, beer, bricks, cattle, chalk, coal, iron, mining, paper, quarrying, steel, and a very long list of finished goods. The industrials might only need connections with the main line system for the despatch of items such as the products of mining, or maybe for bringing materials into the site, going through a manufacturing process, and then despatching the product. Either way, they needed a physical connection. The industrial railway would need to be organised in terms of properly qualified staff and the use of suitable wagons, with the movements to or from the main lines controlled through the signalling system.

The Liverpool & Manchester Railway of 1830 was the first main line as we would recognise it today. It demonstrated the need for separation by purpose, but also compatibility for interworking. The main line network was separately owned, maintained, managed and operated. The Railway Clearing House, established in 1842, played an important part in setting standards and ensuring that each company received a fair proportion of the charges paid by the consignor.

The main lines also provided new and fast-expanding market outlets for the industrial railway traffic. Docks were important origins and destinations, but so too were large towns and their populations, and the growing manufacturing centres.

Would the movements be of such quantities that suggested wagon load use only, train load, or what? This book aims to set out what was happening on industrial railways across the country. Around fifty years ago, the operation was dominated by the National Coal Board (NCB). An informative notice was displayed from 1 January 1947 on the gates of all the 958 collieries then extant: 'This colliery is now managed by the National Coal Board, on behalf of the people.'

The NCB was a statutory corporation created to run the nationalised coal industry in the United Kingdom. It was founded in 1946, continuing until privatisation caused it to be dissolved in 1987 and replaced by British Coal.

From 1958 to 2001 and its own privatisation, the Central Electricity Generating Board (CEGB) was created by Act of Parliament to take responsibility for electricity generation, transmission and bulk supply in England and Wales, but not for overseeing the industry. The NCB dug the coal, the railway brought the coal from the mines to the power stations, the CEGB converted it into electricity, and all were interdependent. Failure of any of these three separate but nationalised industries would cause major problems on a large scale, as from time to time they did. It should perhaps be added that coal was also transported by the inland waterways.

The traditional industrial railway was associated with wagon load traffic, which has long transferred to road. With train load operation, the locomotive bringing the wagons in, or taking them out, often undertakes any shunting needed. But there are still substantial numbers of privately owned diesel shunters around, employed specifically for that purpose.

****

This book offers a cross-section of the various industrial railways in Britain, concentrating on the period from the 1960s through to the 1980s, but with some more recent images. It is arranged on a broadly south to north basis, starting in Cornwall and finishing in Fife. The sections are The Beginnings, South West, South East, London, Midlands, Wales, North West, North East, Cumbria and Scotland.

It does not and indeed could not possibly encompass all industrial railways in its ninety-six pages, but the author hopes that readers will find plenty of topics to interest them. This is about the industrial railway as it was; the preservation movement is not covered.

The photographs by the author and contributors were sometimes taken on visits as part of an invited group, including those organised by the Chartered Institute of Logistics & Transport, the Permanent Way Institution, the Chartered Institution of Railway Operators, the Railway Study Association, and the Industrial Railway Society. Other visits will have been made on an individual basis. Notably, even impromptu visitors were nearly always welcomed by the staff on the ground, to whom much (rather belated) thanks. Around half a century ago there was little formality, and a ride on the locomotive was sometimes forthcoming if you were lucky!

The author has been helped considerably by a number of friends. First my thanks must go to David Young for providing substantial photographic coverage, of Scotland in particular, and also to Peter Ashton. Martin Brailsford was able to give him a lead on some problem areas, while Geoff Robinson has kindly provided his own pictures and those of his late father, G. S. Robinson.

In writing the captions, it was necessary to call on many varied sources, from both books and the web. The author trusts that he has not infringed anyone's copyright in so doing, but this is nearly all factual material. There were far too many individual sources to be listed in what is essentially a picture book, and still leave room for the pictures. He would mention especially the value of the Industrial Railway Society's Pocket Book EL, *British Industrial Locomotives*, 1968. This provided a very useful source of reference when locating industrial railways, and subsequently as a check and sometimes as a correction to his own notes.

There will be errors, as sources don't always agree and interpretations can differ, but hopefully they will be few.

John Glover
Surrey

The Beginnings

Catch Me Who Can was the name given to an early venture into steam locomotives by the Cornishman Richard Trevithick (1771–1833). Running on a circular track near Euston, it was to show that travel by rail was faster than by horse. This is one of a series of plaques displayed on a fence outside Dartford station. (John Glover)

Rocket was the undisputed winner of the competitive trials held at Rainhill in 1829 and became the favoured locomotive for the Liverpool & Manchester Railway, opened in 1830. This was the first proper passenger and goods railway as it would be recognised today. This miniature replica stood outside the one time British Transport Museum at Clapham in south London, seen here on 31 March 1968. (John Glover)

South West

Falmouth Docks & Engineering Company's No. 3 assists in the docking of *MV Mobil Lubchei* on 23 September 1977. The locomotive is a Hawthorn-Leslie 0-4-0ST, No. 3597 of 1926. This is the third largest deepwater harbour in the world. (David Young)

No. 3 is seen at Falmouth Docks. The docks railway opened in 1864 as a consequence of the construction of the Great Western main line from Truro, completed in 1863. The deepwater docks, as they became, covered the considerable area of 150 acres. (G. S. Robinson)

At Par, *Alfred* was the second of two very small but standard gauge 0-4-0ST Bagnall locomotives for use within the harbour area. No. 3058 of 1953 is seen here, shortly before withdrawal, on 23 September 1977. Their diminutive size was dictated by the need to fit under an 8-foot-high bridge beneath the Cornish main line and there were some tight 70-foot-radius curves to be contended with as well. Both engines featured in Revd W. Awdry's 'Railway Series'. (David Young)

The National Coal Board's Peckett No. 1788 of 1929 shunts at the head of the inclined plane to Kilmersdon Colliery, Radstock, on 2 February 1971. Somewhat surreally, it was possible from this same point to see test flights of the supersonic aircraft Concorde above. This was then under construction at nearby Filton. Would the roar of one outlive the chuff of the other? (David Young)

Roads Reconstruction (Quarries) Ltd operated various sites in the area of Vallis Vale, near Frome. A pair of Thomas Hill/Sentinel Vanguard diesel locomotives, Nos 2 (1360/64) and 3 (1524/65), are operating back-to-back with a train for Foster Yeoman on 16 April 1969. This is big business; the construction of Heathrow Terminal 5 required as much as 3 million tons of stone to be supplied – good rail traffic. (John Glover)

Quarrying can be dirty work; this photograph of No. 1 (TH1334/63) shows how much better these Sentinel Vanguard locomotives looked when given a wash and brush up. However, it is one thing to say that, but another to carry out what can be quite time consuming and a decidedly dusty occupation. Industrial railways are unlikely to have mechanical washing facilities. (John Glover)

Out of use for the time being, but able perhaps to return to shunting duties as and when required, No. 3 or S9387/48 was a Sentinel steam locomotive built to that company's distinctive design. The first diesel-powered Sentinel rail (as opposed to road) vehicles appeared in 1959. (John Glover)

The water tank of a deceased Andrew Barclay locomotive (AB1969/03) plus its main frame and wheels made the basis for a weed killing unit. Concoct a means of spraying the track, fill the tank with chemicals and water, couple on a locomotive, turn it all on, and away you go! This was seen at the Vallis Vale sheds on 16 April 1969. (John Glover)

The 1865 branch from Weymouth to Weymouth Quay was used by boat trains from Waterloo for passengers to the Channel Islands and mainland Europe. A Class 33/1 diesel picks its way gingerly through the parked cars on 31 August 1976. This was a tramway operating over a public thoroughfare. Goods traffic ceased in 1972, but passenger services hung on until 1987. The track has now been lifted. (John Glover)

The busy goods branch from Hamorthy Junction on the South Western line west of Poole ran to the land owned by Poole Harbour Commissioners and Hamworthy Quay. The smartly turned out Ruston & Hornsby 0-4-0 diesel in blue and white livery was the property of PD Fuels. It is seen here in September 1977. (John Glover)

South East

Marchwood Military Port in Hampshire is served off the former Fawley branch from Totton. A limited service was run between the three minimal stations on the branch for workers, and otherwise on an as required basis. Seen here is Vanguard Steelman No. 01527 with the first of two Mk2f air-conditioned coaches. It is 10 May 2005. (John Glover)

The passenger halts within Marchwood could not be described as being of anything other than decidedly basic construction. There is not even any form of shelter to keep the rain off intending passengers. But this was far from an ordinary railway service and in any event the last passenger trains ran on 27 November 2013. (John Glover)

A pair of Vanguard 0-4-0s, Nos 01548 and 01541, are seen at Marchwood on 10 May 2005. In the background are some brand new Class 377 units bound for the Brighton main line. These arrived from Derby before the TOC was able to cope with them, so the MoD helpfully offered accommodation. (John Glover)

The goods brake van is now effectively extinct, though the Army maintained a modest fleet at Marchwood in 2005. This is WGM4809. The guard, riding in the van, was able to apply braking power to help the enginemen when needed on unbraked trains – that is when the locomotive and the van were the only sources of brake power. The intermediate wagons had brakes that could be applied, but by hand only. This was clearly less than ideal with a moving train. (John Glover)

This is the London & South Western Railway's B4 class 0-4-0T locomotive No. 30096 *Corrall Queen* of 1891 in steam. The location is Corrall's Dibles Wharf, Southampton, on 17 December 1972. No. 30096 was shortly to move to the Bluebell Railway. The positions of the lamps on the front buffer beam indicate that it is hauling an express passenger service, but of this there was no sign. (David Young)

A remarkable four of the eight members of South Eastern's P class 0-6-0T locomotives have survived the cutters' torch. They were introduced in 1909. No. 753 (BR No. 31556) was later bought by Hodson's Flour Mill and named *Pride of Sussex*. It is seen here at Rolvenden in October 1970. (John Glover)

The Bowaters Pulp & Paper Mills on the Isle of Sheppey had a standard gauge track, which was a private siding connected to the Sheerness branch. On it stands SE&CR P class 0-6-0T *Pioneer ll* (BR No. 31178). It was later sold to the Bluebell Railway, where it was painted black, lined out in yellow, and given the fetching name of *Primrose*. (John Glover)

Jubilee was a Bagnall 0-4-0ST built for Bowaters in 1936, seen here in steam at Ridham shed on 6 July 1968. Between them, the two standard gauge locomotives kept the show on the road for traffic to and from the national network. This was, after all, only a very short length of track. (John Glover)

Bowaters were known particularly for their extensive 2-foot 6-inch narrow gauge steam-worked system. This conveyed Scandinavian imports of wood pulp from Ridham Dock on the River Swale to their premises. Here, on 6 July 1968, a Bagnall product of 1940 0-6-2T *Superb* receives a wash and brush up from its crew. (John Glover)

The Bowaters system conveyed large quantities of paper products, as is indicated by the mound behind the train at Ridham Dock. This is headed by 0-6-2T *Conqueror*, built by W. G. Bagnall in 1922. The spark arrestor chimney will be noted – a desirable device for paper products when steam traction is used. It is 6 July 1968. (John Glover)

Bagnall 0-6-2T *Superb* is captured backing onto its train at Ridham Dock on 6 July 1968. Bowaters had a considerable fleet of steam locomotives, of which relatively few would be in use at any one time. This reflected changing requirements over time, but also what could be the irregular arrivals of ships and the discharge of their cargoes. (John Glover)

This curious machine was a four-wheeled battery electric vehicle, dating back to 1921. It was built for Bowaters by English Electric, works No. 515. It is seen here at Ridham Dock on 6 July 1968. Named (nicknamed?) *The Tank*, it survived until the closing of the railway forty-eight years later. (John Glover)

At the Sittingbourne shed, the fire is dropped from Kerr Stuart's 1924 0-4-2ST *Melior* on 4 October 1969. The railway dated from 1906 and reached its maximum length of around 10 miles in 1936. The system was closed completely in 1969 and, until the end, some passenger vehicles were available for the carriage of staff. Part of the line was then leased to the Locomotive Club of Great Britain as the Sittingbourne & Kemsley Light Railway. (John Glover)

This was the final passenger train run under Bowaters management on 4 October 1969, as a special for Locomotive Club of Great Britain members. It is seen here at Kemsley, in less than ideal weather, en route for Sittingbourne. Goods operations by Bowaters continued until 25 October 1969. (John Glover)

The National Coal Board purchased a number of British Railways diesel shunters. Class 12 No. 15224 was an ex-Southern Railway machine built at Ashford works to a design by Bulleid/ English Electric. It dated from 1949. It was photographed on 18 August 1981 in Snowdown colliery yard. Rail traffic here had by then ceased, and the colliery itself closed in 1987. (John Glover)

Former BR Class 11 No. 12131, an LMS Fairburn/English Electric design, was built at Darlington in 1952. After a career in East Anglian yards, it was sold to the National Coal Board in 1969. It too found itself at Snowdon colliery on 18 August 1981. Although the main line railways were experimenting with diesel shunters, their results appeared remarkably similar. (John Glover)

Work on the site of what was to become the National Coal Board's Chislet Colliery began in 1914, with the first coal extracted in 1918. Steam traction was later replaced by diesel and this view shows Andrew Barclay diesel shunter, works No. 382 of 1950, at work in the yard. The colliery itself closed on 25 January 1969. (John Glover)

The British Railways Sheerness branch from Sittingbourne has a mile-long west-facing industrial branch from the intermediate station of Queenborough on the Isle of Sheppey. It ended on a pier on the River Swale. Former British Railways diesel shunters hauled the traffic of Shipbreakers Ltd, whether as scrap or for shipment. Here, an anonymous Class 04 is seen on the pier on 25 March 1981. (John Glover)

Scrapping was, or easily could be, big business. The locomotive in this view is more than dwarfed by the crane above it. The location is at Hope Reach, just short of where the River Swale meets the Medway. A location such as this could be used for both import and export traffic. (John Glover)

A train of bogie flats hauled by an unidentified diesel shunter heads towards Queenborough and the steel rolling mills on 25 March 1981. Railways carry big loads when compared with a road vehicle, but ships can carry much larger loads still. This was always an interesting railway, as one never quite knew what to expect. (John Glover)

In the area of Dartford were many of the cement plants of Associated Portland Cement Manufacturers Ltd (APCM), later Blue Circle. These included Snodland and the largest at Swanscombe. In the Holborough chalk quarry at Snodland could be found 0-4-0ST *Tumulus*, works No. 7813 of 1954 from Robert Stephenson & Hawthorn. It is October 1970. (John Glover)

At the nearby Holborough works of APCM was *Longfield*, a Peckett 0-4-0ST with outside cylinders, No. 1747 of 1928. It is seen here in October 1970, by which time the North Kent cement industry had evolved to become the largest centre for the production of cement in Europe. The works here would close in 1973. (John Glover)

Hornpipe was APCM's Peckett 0-4-0ST No. 1756 of 1928, effectively a twin to *Longfield*. Between them, these two locomotives were responsible for many years for handling all the rail traffic at Holborough works. Notably, coal mostly came by rail, although there was also a capacious wharf on the River Medway. (John Glover)

APCM Swanscombe had seven steam locomotives. Six were built by Hawthorn Leslie in the interwar period, plus one more (with non-interchangeable parts) by Robert Stephenson & Hawthorn in 1948. All were 0-4-0STs. This view of 6 July 1968 shows the depth of the quarrying that took place here, and a train below headed by No. 3. (John Glover)

Regular coaling is a necessity with steam traction, which is seen here being carried out on No. 4 on 27 April 1968. Or maybe one of the others. As most of the locomotive water tanks, which carried the locomotive number on their sides, were identical, it didn't matter too much if parts were exchanged for those of another of the class during overhaul. (John Glover)

Swanscombe's No. 1 has an even coating of dust from the cement. It is 6 July 1968. It would seem that this was a problem for all the communities in the area, which was not well received by the local ladies hanging their washing out to dry. However, these works did provide substantial employment. (John Glover)

A member of the locomotive crew boards a much cleaner No. 3 going about its duties in APCM's Swanscombe quarries. The 0-4-0 wheel arrangement with saddle tank above was popular for industrial locomotives. There was after all a considerable incentive to buy something that worked 'off the peg', rather than go to the expense and uncertainties of having something designed especially for your business. (John Glover)

Notable at APCM Swanscombe were the two wagon hoists, one of which is shown here in this view of 6 July 1968. These were similar to the mechanical coaling plants that were used on the main line steam railways. The wagons are hoisted, to be unloaded by gravity, the empties then being returned to ground level. The train can then be reformed for return to the workings. (John Glover)

Swanscombe's No. 3 brings a loaded train from the works site towards the wagon hoists for unloading. As can be seen, these can be quite large and therefore heavy blocks of material and need to be treated accordingly. It is 27 April 1968. The Swanscombe plant as a whole was closed in 1990. (John Glover)

The Longmoor Military Railway was built by the Royal Engineers, to be used as a training ground for the Army in the construction and operation of railways. The 0-6-0ST *Woolmer* was built by Avonside of Bristol in 1910, works No. 1572. It was operational at Longmoor until 1953. *Woolmer* was then mounted on a plinth outside the main building as what might be termed a sort of long service award. It is seen here on 28 September 1968. (John Glover)

Sat side by side with *Woolmer* at Longmoor was the 0-4-2WT *Gazelle*. This diminutive locomotive was built in 1893 by Dodman of King's Lynn for a private client. Its size can be judged by the figures of David Young (left) and Peter Ashton (right) on the footplate. It came into the possession of the then War Department through the latter's acquisition of the Shropshire & Montgomeryshire Railway in 1941. (John Glover)

General Lord Robertson was a Sentinel diesel hydraulic 0-8-0 locomotive, built new in 1963 for use at Longmoor. The design allowed shunting staff to ride on the locomotive in a protected position, but with quick access to the track as needed. This is one of those features that is easy enough to incorporate at the design stage, but very difficult to add subsequently. (John Glover)

The War Department had a need for large locomotives, mostly 2-8-0s, but also 2-10-0s for use in Europe as well as in Britain. *Gordon*, No. 600, was one of the 2-10-0s and was built by the North British Locomotive Company in 1943. It is seen here on 28 September 1968 on the bridge crossing the yard at Longmoor Downs with a train from Liss. (John Glover)

The badge of the Royal Corps of Transport (RCT) is included on the nameplate of No. 600 *Gordon*. The inscription reads 'Honi-Soit-Qui-Mal-Y-Pense' or 'Shame on anyone who thinks evil of it'. The RCT was formed in 1965 to manage all matters in relation to the transport of men and materials for the Army and others. In 1993 it became part of the Royal Logistic Corps. (John Glover)

A trip on an open day might be from Longmoor Downs to Liss and back, or it could be used by passengers arriving by British Rail trains at Liss. Here Army diesel hydraulic 0-6-0 No. 8219 (459319/61), built by Ruston & Hornsby, approaches Longmoor Downs with a single but decidedly full ex-BR brake second compartment vehicle. (John Glover)

WD196 *Errol Lonsdale*, seen here at Longmoor Downs on 28 September 1968, is one of the large numbers of Austerity 0-6-0 saddle tanks built for the War Department by Hunslet of Leeds and their various contractors. Subsequent orders came from the National Coal Board and industry generally. Delivery was from 1943 to 1964 for a total of 485 locomotives – this was net of any rebuilds. (John Glover)

WD 878 *Basra* was a 350-hp 0-6-0 diesel electric shunter built at Derby in 1945 by the London, Midland & Scottish Railway to their own designs. Well over one thousand similar and very successful machines were built by or on behalf of British Railways. Construction continued until 1963 and many are still in service on National Rail and with industrial systems nationwide. 'Simple, economical to build and cheap to run.' (John Glover)

Ruston & Hornsby 0-6-0 No. 8227 *Hassan* was one of a fleet of this company's diesel shunters built for the Ministry of Defence in the early 1960s. The design was based on the similar Class 07 then being delivered to British Rail for use in Southampton Docks, but with the engine uprated to 400 hp. (John Glover)

The Army had a number of coaching vehicles which could be pressed into service to provide for the transport of injured service personnel and perhaps to provide an element of medical care while under way. Three vehicles of this nature are seen at the Longmoor open day in 1969. Should such vehicles be built specially for such purposes, or is the selective refurbishment of elderly coaching stock, giving it a new lease of life, more sensible? (John Glover)

This is 'Austerity' 0-6-0ST No. 118 *Brussels*, tucked away at the back of the premises and hiding the fact that it is not, perhaps, in the most presentable condition. This was one of a Hudswell Clarke build, works No. 1782 of 1945, which was not completed until the end of hostilities were at least in sight. (John Glover)

The successful loading of a tank onto a railway vehicle is being demonstrated at the Longmoor open day on 28 September 1969. Accuracy in positioning is essential, but so too can be the speed at which it is done. It is also important to take into account where the centre of gravity of the tank will lie and how that might interact with the rail vehicles onto which it is being loaded. (John Glover)

On display at Longmoor was the Schwellenpflug, a form of plough, which was intended to be used by Germans forces in the face of a pursuing enemy. First, a hole is dug in the track. The hook-shaped plough, which needed to be extremely strong, is then lowered into it. The plough is then attached to one or perhaps two locomotives and hauled along. In the process, the sleepers are destroyed, and the track becomes unusable. (John Glover)

Even ungated level crossings will need protection of some sort. Here, a couple of soldiers are doing the honours as 0-6-0ST WD196 *Errol Lonsdale* crosses a road near Longmoor Downs on 31 October 1969. The evident dangers of level crossings became obvious from the early days and this resulted in legislation for the protection of road users as early as the Highways Act 1830. (John Glover)

Eventually, the Longmoor Military Railway was seen as surplus to Army requirements, and the closing ceremony took place on 31 October 1969. The 2-10-0 No. 600 *Gordon* is about to haul the very last train from Longmoor Downs on its fourteen-minute journey to Oakhanger, then back again. And that will be that! (John Glover)

London

At Tolworth on the Chessington branch, a coal concentration depot was built. After closure, the land was used for other bulk industries such as aggregates. Two Drewry diesel shunters of Class 04, formerly Nos D2246 and D2310, but no longer in BR usage, are seen awaiting the next call on their services on 30 March 1977. (John Glover)

The wholly underground Post Office Railway of 6.5 miles and 2 foot gauge was used for the carriage of mails across central London. The original nine stations included Paddington and Liverpool Street (both main line) and the principal sorting office of Mount Pleasant (near Farringdon). It was opened on 3 December 1927 and closed finally on 31 May 2003. This view of a Mount Pleasant platform was taken in March 1988. (John Glover)

This view of Mount Pleasant shows that there were separate parts of each platform for loading and unloading, while a through track allowed trains to bypass the platforms if there was no reason to stop. The headroom in the running tunnels was severely restricted and staff were not carried on the trains. The loading gauge was described as 'Custom'. (John Glover)

Most of the operational rolling stock for MailRail originated from around 1930, but in 1980 a further build took place. This is one of these later Greenbat/Hunslet vehicles in the depot area. Other changes saw a centralised control system replace that at each station, but by the late 1990s only four stations remained. (John Glover)

There was but one depot-cum-maintenance area on the Post Office Railway, situated at Mount Pleasant. It is seen here in March 1988. The narrow gauge of 2 feet may be noticed and the way in which running rails and tracks were distinguished by colour to keep staff safe from moving vehicles. (John Glover)

An Avonside 0-6-0ST built in 1933, works No. 2068, *Robert,* lived an uneventful life shunting at the premises of Staveley Coal & Iron in Northants. Retired in 1969, it then had a whole string of owners before becoming the property of the London Borough of Newham in 1999. *Robert* is seen here on a temporary stand outside Stratford station in October 2001. (John Glover)

London Underground's 0-6-0 Pannier tank No. L90 is stood just short of a water column at Neasden on 6 June 1971. It gives the impression that it is eying up the column up and waiting, just a little impatiently, for opening time. The locomotive was built in 1930 by North British Loco for the Great Western Railway and given the running number of 7760. It was sold to London Transport in 1961. (Peter Ashton)

Seen here on shed at London Transport, Neasden, on 8 November 1969, are former Great Western Pannier tanks No. L90, formerly No. 7711 and built by Kerr Stuart, and No. L94, which was No. 7752, a North British Locomotive Co. product. Both were built in 1930. On 6 June 1971, No. L84 would haul a demonstration special from Barbican to Neasden to mark the end of steam operations on the Underground. (Peter Ashton)

Battery locomotives were built to tube loading gauge, giving them an ability to travel to almost all parts of the Underground system. The fleet size is around thirty in total. On 30 June 2009 Upminster Underground platforms see Nos L28 and L47. L28 is from the Metro-Cammell build of 1965 while L47 was built by BREL Doncaster in 1974. The main body parts of the BREL locomotives had been painted blue. (John Glover)

Extensive construction work was carried out at Stonebridge Park to accommodate the Princess Royal Distribution Centre between the main lines and the DC lines. It would have seven enclosed platforms and would be located in an ideal place for network access. Sadly, Royal Mail decided that transport by rail was not to be pursued. Here, construction work is underway by the Trackwork company using a four-wheeled Planet locomotive on 28 February 1996. (John Glover)

Midlands

The Pitstone works of Tunnel Portland Cement Ltd were situated at the north end of Tring cutting. Their extensive sidings had the disadvantage of feeding both into and out of the West Coast fast lines, which is not very welcome when line capacity is at a premium. Seen here shunting on 18 May 1983 is their four-wheeled diesel hydraulic Rolls-Royce/Sentinel No. 3, works No. 19264. It was built in 1966. (John Glover)

The Nassington Barrowden Mining Company had a pair of their 0-6-0ST locomotives in use on 6 July 1970. This is *Jacks Green* outside the shed at Nassington. It was built by Hunslet of Leeds in 1939, works No. 1953. The locomotive was used for hauling iron ore tipplers out of the quarries, three or four at a time, and taking them to the dispatch sidings. (David Young)

Ring Haw was also a Hunslet build, of 1940. Works No. 1982, it was seen in the Nassington ironstone quarries on 6 July 1970. This is an inside cylinder 0-6-0ST, which on that day had a decidedly unusual load of passengers from the Industrial Railway Society in the wagons. The quarries were closed later that year. (David Young)

Stourport-on-Severn power station was displaying its Peckett 0-4-0ST (1893/36) on 9 June 1969. This went by the obscure name of *W.A. No. 2*. One can only hope that its mechanical condition was rather better than its external appearance. Coal was received here by barge as well as by rail, but electricity generation ceased in 1984. (John Glover)

This is the tipping dock for Isebrook Quarry of Thomas E. Gray of Burton Latimer (near Kettering) on 6 February 1971. The locomotive is on 2-foot gauge track, with wagons containing silica sand being tipped into standard gauge wagons. These could only be moved within the site; in this case, to the nearby works. The locomotive, works No. 5881 of 1935, is from Motor Rail Ltd's Simplex Works at Bedford. (David Young)

The Sentinel Waggon Works company of Shrewsbury built a remarkable selection of steam lorries and locomotives, followed by diesel-powered versions, including buses. Seen at Isebrook Quarry, Burton Latimer, on 27 February 1971 is Thomas E. Gray's *Musketeer*. This was a four-wheeled locomotive with a vertical boiler, dating from 1946 with works number 9369. The quarry closed in 1989. (David Young)

Near Brookfield sidings, Corby, on 23 June 1973, is one of fourteen Hawthorn Leslie 0-6-0Ts for Stewarts & Lloyds. This is No. 21 (works No. 3931, built in 1938), seen here at the head of a last day of steam special for the Industrial Railway Society on a tour of the Corby ironstone quarries. The striking buttercup yellow livery, with red wheels and motion, was applied generally to their steam fleet. Steel making here ceased progressively from 1981. (David Young)

At the rear of the Stewarts & Lloyds train at Corby is their No. 28, a former British Rail Class 14 locomotive No. D9547, one of a class of fifty-six diesel hydraulics built at Swindon works in 1964/65. A limited output of 650 hp, coupled with a 40 mph maximum and a lack of ability to work in multiple, meant that British Rail had sold or scrapped the entire class by the end of 1970. (David Young)

Burton-on-Trent was well known for its breweries. This is the Bass locomotive shed, showing what extensive premises these were. Unfortunately, none of the locomotives were identified. The Bass company alone had enough work to keep twelve locomotives busy over their 20 miles of line, to say nothing of the 120 horses used for shunting (but this was in 1901). Some fourteen firms in Burton were then involved in the brewing business. (G. S. Robinson)

Bass had the largest private rail network in Britain, both at Burton-upon-Trent and elsewhere. The Worthington company merged with Bass in 1927, but the Worthington brewery closed in 1965. The company's Bagnall 0-4-0ST No. 16, works No. 2103 and built in 1923, was prepared for display at some time in the mid-1960s. (G. S. Robinson)

Burton-upon-Trent was notorious for the large number of road level crossings, around twenty-four in total, which saw intensive use for the breweries' railway traffic. A petition against the nuisance of railways in the streets was organised as early as 1859. Here, a Midland Railway-style signal box protects a crossing. These became even more well known when one featured in a painting by the Salford artist L. S. Lowry in 1969, complete with a brewery train. (G. S. Robinson)

This blue 0-4-0 diesel locomotive was built by the local company Baguley of Burton-on-Trent, works No. 3590, in 1962. The customer was Bass Breweries, who gave it fleet number 11. The Bass triangle on its front may be noted. The engine had a modest 107-hp power output and was sold on when the brewery railways closed. (Geoff Robinson)

With a smart red finish, Bass No. 12, a Rolls-Royce/Sentinel, is seen in the vicinity of the Shobnal brewery. Note the well-placed steps up to the locomotive. This four-wheeled diesel hydraulic carried a works number of 10003 and was built in 1959. (Geoff Robinson)

All proper railways need a suitable vehicle for the transport of top brass. The Bass Directors' Saloon is partially hidden in its shed, but awaiting its next call of duty. There may not have been too many of these to come, as all the brewery railways were closed by the end of 1967. (G. S. Robinson)

The Central Electricity Generating Board's Meaford power station stood south of Stoke-on-Trent, between Barlaston and Stone. The locomotive is *No.2 Muriel*, an 0-4-0ST built by Bagnall's of Stafford in 1945, works No. 2829. It is 7 June 1969. The huge size of the cooling towers relative to the train is only too apparent. The power station opened in 1957, closing in 1990. (John Glover)

The National Coal Board's Cadley Hill colliery, Swadlingcote, south Derbyshire, was established in 1861. Deep coal mining here ceased in 1988, though some opencast working continued until 1997. Railway shunting, as seen here on 17 February 1973, was being carried out by *Progress*, an 0-6-0ST built by Robert Stephenson & Hawthorn, works No. 7298 in 1946. (David Young)

Wales

The Richard, Thomas & Baldwin's Spencer steelworks at Llanwern saw large quantities of coke oven slag being moved. It is October 1966. Whether this can truly be described as rail transport is perhaps debatable, though the vehicle is definitely supported by something that closely resembles a railway. The clearances needed though are considerably different from those of the national system. (John Glover)

There were two Central Electricity Generating Board coal-fired power stations in Newport (Monmouthshire), Uskmouth A (now demolished) and Uskmouth B. Seen here on 4 January 1969, Hawthorn-Leslie 0-4-0ST *Faraday* was the then resident shunter. The locomotive was built in 1932, works No. 3793. The power station has been closed since 2015 with the intention of converting it to biomass. (John Glover)

This is the National Coal Board's Merthyr Vale colliery on 31 March 1970. As dieselisation progressed, British Railways Western Region were only too keen to get rid of their large fleet of 0-6-0 Pannier tanks. No. 9600 was built at Swindon in 1945 and is seen here in NCB ownership. Unusually, it retained its BR number and lion emblem, while still sporting its unlined black livery. (John Glover)

The National Coal Board's locomotive shed at Mountain Ash sees *Lord Camrose*, which was named after a local dignitary. This was an Avonside 0-6-0ST locomotive, works No. 2008 of 1930, awaiting attention on 25 September 1968. The growth of collieries resulted in a local population increase from 1,600 in 1841 to 11,400 by 1871. By 1859, they were supporting twelve pubs. (John Glover)

On 4 July 1970, the NCB's Andrew Barclay 0-4-0ST *Glan Dulais*, works No. 1109 of 1907, took a Branch Line Society special from Pontardulais up the Dulais Valley to the end of the branch at Graig Merthyr. Travel was in a set of four Paddy wagons. The line was closed in 1978. (John Glover)

On 21 March 1970, a special hauled by ex-Great Western 0-6-0PT No. 7754 was run by the National Coal Board from Talywain Crossing (Golynos Junction) to Blaenserchan Colliery and back. This was immediately before the line's closure. As seen here, the train consisted of open mineral wagons followed by covered fruit vans (used as Paddy train coaches) and a second engine. The journey time was thirty-five minutes each way. (David Young)

The surface location of pit shafts might be decidedly inconvenient, so transport for the men might be laid on. These four wagons at Abersychon, seen here on 4 January 1969, were used for such purposes. The accommodation consisted of bench seating around the internal walls and nothing else. It is perhaps unnecessary to state that there was no first class. (John Glover)

North West

This is the Central Electricity Generating Board's Stuart Street power station in Manchester on 2 March 1969. The locomotive is an outside cylindered 0-4-0ST with neither name nor fleet number, though it was understood to be known as *Irwell No 3*. The power station opened in 1900, closing in 1975. (John Glover)

The 0-4-0ST locomotive was a standard design from Hudswell Clarke of Leeds, works No. 1672 of 1937. The locomotive did look rather older than its origin in the 1930s, but it was in steam. If it was economical in its use of resources, easy to maintain and worked well, what more should its owners want? (John Glover)

Collyhurst Carriage Sidings were situated a short distance east of Manchester Victoria station. Former Midland Railway 'Jinty' 0-6-0T was withdrawn from Lostock Hall as No. 47564 in March 1965 and converted into a stationary boiler for carriage heating. With side tanks removed, it became service stock No. 2022, seen here on 5 March 1969. It survived in this role until at least 1972. (John Glover)

CEGB Hartshead power station, about 1.5 miles north-east of Stalybridge, was served by sidings on the Micklesford relief line. These were built in 1932 for 130 wagons, so that the power station coal could be transported by enclosed conveyor belt across the railway, the River Tame and the Huddersfield Narrow Canal. This is 0-4-0ST No. 2 (RSHN7661/50). (John Glover)

This fireless locomotive at Hartshead is a Hawthorn Leslie, works No. 3805 of 1932, which was seen here on 2 March 1969. The power station opened in 1926 and closed on 29 October 1979, but the last section of railway serving it had closed in 1976. Hartshead had been partly converted to oil firing in the 1960s. (John Glover)

The Manchester Ship Canal company purchased two diesel electric shunting locomotives from Hudswell Clarke. The first of was No. 4001 (D1075/59) and was given the name of *Alnwick Castle*. It had a 400-hp engine and a top speed of 15 mph; it is seen here in March 1971. (John Glover)

An industry display in Salford Docks on 9 May 1971 saw one of the Manchester Ship Canal Company's fleet of Sentinel/Rolly-Royce four-wheeled diesel hydraulics, No. DH29 (works No. 10243 of 1966), on display. These were procured as part of the MSC's dieselisation plan, but the railway traffic was declining. (John Glover)

Chadderton B power station, owned by the Central Electricity Generating Board, was opened officially on 8 July 1955. This locomotive, an 0-4-0 diesel mechanical shunter built by John Fowler in 1949, works No. 4210011, was just plain No. 1 in the fleet at Chadderton. The date is 2 March 1969. (John Glover)

Usefully, the Chadderton site, near Oldham, was close to the Calder Valley line from Manchester to Rochdale. It was thus suitable for coal to be delivered by railway. *Chadderton No 2* was an 0-4-0ST built by Andrew Barclay, works No. 2367 of 1955, but on 2 March 1969 it seems to have acquired the unofficial name of *Bob*. That more personal title does trip off the tongue rather more easily! (John Glover)

The Agecroft power station of the Central Electricity Generating Board had three 0-4-0STs built by Robert Stephenson & Hawthorn. This picture shows *Agecroft No 1*, works No. 7416 of 1948, plus the one which never acquired a name, works No. 7681 of 1951. The three locomotives were identical, to all intents and purposes. (John Glover)

It is the bright but frosty day of 30 January 1969 and *Agecroft No 2* (7485/48) is seen with a line of wagons at the power station unloading point. However, the building of a conveyor belt direct from Agecroft colliery dispensed with the need for much of the rail traffic, and this ceased altogether in September 1981. The power station itself was closed in 1993. (John Glover)

Rail access to Kearsley power station was by a private line leading to the sidings. This was steeply graded at 1 in 22, which was in itself a good reason for choosing electric traction. One of the four 0-4-4-0 overhead electric locomotives (probably No. 3) is using the link, running light engine from the Down side of the Manchester to Bolton line. It passed beneath those tracks, turning back as it did so to reach the power station sidings. It is June 1970. (John Glover)

This Kearsley system was electrified at 500v DC overhead. It was run using four similar electric locomotives, built between 1927 and 1945. They were not identical; building them over a period of eighteen years made sure of that. This photograph was taken in June 1970 and shows No. 3 (7078/44) from Robert Stephenson & Hawthorn as successors to Hawthorn Leslie, with its wagons being unloaded. (John Glover)

This is Kearsley's No. 1 from Robert Stephenson & Hawthorn, works No. 3682 of 1927, approaching. The background is, or perhaps was, a typical industrial landscape of the area. The power station on the right is probably Agecroft. It is October 1970. (John Glover)

Health and safety may seem like a concern of recent times, but this June 1970 example is now half a century old. It is perhaps obvious to many that shunting is something to be careful about, but it doesn't do any harm to say so. Trains cannot stop instantly; even if the driver of Kearsley's No. 1 sees you, he may not be able to stop in time. (John Glover)

This is the backup diesel locomotive on the Kearsley power station site. Seen here in June 1970, this was Fowler diesel mechanical 0-4-0 No. 1 (not to be confused with the plain No. 1 of the electric locomotives). The diesel was works No. 4210078, of 1952. The power station itself closed in 1982. (John Glover)

The Astley Green colliery site always seemed to be brimming with activity. On nationalisation in 1947 it employed 1,375 people below ground and 561 above. The motive power was provided by 'Austerity' type 0-6-0ST locomotives built in Leeds. The oldest was *Harry*, built in 1944 by Hudswell Clarke & Co., works No. 1776, which is seen here in commendably clean condition taking water on 21 December 1968. (John Glover)

Coaling was carried out with the aid of a skip, seen here with the rear end of *Harry* (HC 1776/44) on 21 December 1968. Coal and especially water are essential elements of running a successful steam railway, and to have them easily and quickly available is a substantial benefit. (John Glover)

Stanley (3302/45) carries out some shunting of National Coal Board wagons. This is one of the engines fitted with a Giesl ejector – note the unusual chimney. It was invented in 1951 by the Austrian Dr Giesl to improve blastpipe suction draught and make better use of energy. It was, however, rather too late in the day for steam traction generally. (John Glover)

Here, *Respite* (works No. 3696 of 1950) and *Stanley* have at least twenty-five fully loaded 16-ton mineral wagons behind them as they get their train underway on 27 November 1969. Astley Green colliery opened in 1912 and closed in 1970. On its site, the Lancashire Mining Museum has the last locally remaining pithead gear, but the extensive railway sidings and most of the buildings and have now disappeared under a housing estate. (John Glover)

It was a hard pull up towards Walkden for the line from Astley Green, once away from the canal. *Warrior*, a Hunslet Austerity (3823/54) built for the National Coal Board, is, however, taking it in its stride. This route would take it past the locomotive workshops for the area. (John Glover)

At the National Coal Board's Bickershaw Colliery on 16 June 1971, the Hunslet Austerity (HE3831 of 1955, and thus a relatively late build) is taking a train of wagons towards the main line interchange. Its more or less identical twin was named, as one might guess, *Hurricane*, but was not to be seen on this occasion. (John Glover)

Something like 300,000 16-ton mineral wagons were built for the movement of coal. These had a wheelbase of 9 feet, a length of 16 feet 6 inches, two side doors and one end door. The vast majority had hand brakes only. Here at Bickershaw Colliery on 16 June 1971 is a line of them, owned by the National Coal Board. The white X on the sides indicates colliery ownership, though they perhaps looked rather better in dark blue than the light grey used by BR. (John Glover)

The Central Electricity Generating Board's Huncoat power station used a fleet of three fireless locomotives – 0-4-0s Nos 1 and 2 built by Bagnall in 1951 and No 3, the rather older and larger 0-6-0 from Hawthorn Leslie, dating from 1929. This shows No. 1 (left) and No. 2 (right) at work here on 2 August 1968. A half mile branch connected Huncoat colliery to the power station. (John Glover)

Fireless locomotives take steam from a pipe in the works area, sufficient to allow them to perform local movements before they need recharging. No fire on the locomotive meant no risk of external fire either, but they also depended on an available reservoir of high-pressure steam. This is Huncoat's No. 3, repairing to the shed on 2 August 1968. The power station closed in 1984. (John Glover)

Yates Duxbury paper mills at Heap Bridge, near Bury, had the distinction of running the last steam-operated private industry railway. Perhaps unsurprisingly, that did not include those of the National Coal Board. This is Andrew Barclay 0-4-0ST, works No. 945 of 1904, seen here on 5 March 1969. (John Glover)

A little newer than the Barclay was the 0-4-0ST *May*, a Peckett works No. 1370 of 1915. The date is 17 June 1971. These sidings led off the Lancashire & Yorkshire line between Bury and Rochdale. The Yates Duxbury railway closed in 1974, and the mills themselves in 1981. (John Glover)

A rear view of the Peckett *May*, which was often to be found in this prominent position at Yates Duxbury. The Peckett company's strengths were in the manufacture of industrial and shunting locomotives of the 0-4-0 or 0-6-0 types. They were based in Bristol and the company folded in 1961. (John Glover)

This is one of the Port of Preston Authority's vans for internal use within the docks only. Labelled P2C, it was photographed on 27 November 1968. That similar vehicles of such a modest size and capacity were commonplace on the railways of Britain, to be shunted in huge marshalling yards only recently built, is a reminder of the updating of freight operations then still outstanding. (John Glover)

North East

The Middleton Railway has a number of claims to fame, not least that it has been working continuously since 1758. For this, it was the first railway to be granted powers by Act of Parliament. On 22 August 1971, what was British Railways Departmental locomotive No. 54 is seen with an open wagon and a goods brake van full of customers. (John Glover)

Horsepower on the Middleton Railway was later replaced by steam and coal was the main traffic carried. Since 1960, it has been run by volunteers, with freight services continuing until 1983. This steam locomotive was built by the Sentinel Waggon Works in 1933, works No. 8837, for the London & North Eastern Railway, No. 59. It became British Railways No. 68153. (John Glover)

It is not often that a motorway under construction has to bridge a heritage railway. On the top is what would become the M621, below the Middleton Railway, which then predated it by 213 years. When the engineer in charge asked the cheapest way to cross the railway, he was reputedly told a level crossing! It is hard to imagine all this happening had the railway not been there already. (John Glover)

Trackwork Ltd is a specialist rail infrastructure company undertaking construction and engineering services, track maintenance and renewals. It was founded in 1976 and is based in Doncaster. Here a four-wheeled Planet locomotive is seen shunting at Thornaby. (John Glover)

This Andrew Barclay 0-6-0ST, owned by the National Coal Board, is at work at Shotton Colliery, near Peterlee, in County Durham. It is 3 July 1971. This locomotive, works No. 1015, dated from 1904. Unusually, Shotton Colliery is also the name of the village itself. Coal production started in 1834 but there was a break between 1877 and 1900. Final closure came in September 1972. (David Young)

By the time this photograph was taken in 1971, Andrew Barclay's Shotton Colliery saddle tank was already sixty-seven years old. However, the colliery itself only had another fifteen months to go before closure. Steam traction had its benefits and drawbacks, but its ability to keep going to a ripe old age could certainly work in its favour. (David Young)

Swalwell Disposal Point for the National Coal Board's Opencast Executive was in County Durham. Here, on 9 May 1970, is Austerity 0-6-0ST No. 75167. It dated from 1944 and was built by William Bagnall, works No. 2755. The locomotive belonged to Johnson's Ltd and is attending to a derailed wagon. If such wagons were the property of British Railways and appeared to be ok, a call out and the associated charges might be avoided. (David Young)

This Andrew Barclay 0-4-0ST with outside cylinders, works No. 1659 and built in 1920, was delivered new to the East Tanfield colliery. Its use included hauling wagons to the River Tyne for onward transport by water. Named *Stanley*, it became No. 32 of the NCB's North Durham Area's fleet. It is seen here as it was in September 1972. (John Glover)

A fleet of five works locomotives was built by Brush Traction with Rolls-Royce engines for the Tyne & Wear Passenger Transport Executive. Nos WL1–WL5, each with a maximum speed of 50 km/h date from 1977/78. This is No. WL1 with a wiring train for the forthcoming Metro service on 17 April 1980. It is in the outer line platform at Whitley Bay, headed towards Tynemouth. (John Glover)

Electrified industrial railways were something of a rarity, but such was the case with the Harton Electric Railway in South Tyneside. Latterly, this once extensive 550v DC system was confined to linking St Hilda's siding with Harton Low Staithes on the River Tyne via a very restricted tunnel. Here, English Electric/Baguley No. 15 2600/59 is seen at Westoe Colliery, South Shields, on 13 April 1980. It closed in 1989. (John Glover)

Earsdon is where the National Coal Board line crossed the British Railways Blyth & Tyne, all supervised by the British Railways signal box of that name. English Electric Type 3 No. D6756 (later 37.056) is propelling a goods brake van westwards towards Gosforth. It is September 1970. (John Glover)

This 0-6-2T No. 42 was constructed by Robert Stephenson & Co. at Darlington in 1920, works No. 3801. It is seen here in the shed at NCB Philadelphia on 13 January 1969. This is one of seven broadly similar locomotives built for the Lambton Railway by three different companies between 1904 and 1934. The rounded cab profile was to allow them to work through a narrow bored tunnel at the Port of Sunderland. (John Glover)

Another Lambton locomotive from this series was No. 30. This was built by Kitson & Co. of Leeds in 1920, works No. 4532. It is seen here outside the National Coal Board's Philadelphia workshops and running shed on 13 January 1969. A further five similar locomotives came, second hand, from the Great Western Railway, being no longer needed in the South Wales valleys. (John Glover)

Robert Stephenson & Hawthorn's 'Austerity' 0-6-0ST, fleet No. 10, was fast becoming no more than a memory. The action is taking place at NCB Philadelphia on 13 January 1969. The works number was 7294, with construction taking place in 1945. Something like 48 tons of scrap metal will become available for other purposes. (John Glover)

From a high vantage point at Backworth in June 1970, NCB No. 48, an 0-6-0ST built by Hunslet, No. 2864 in 1943, can be seen propelling 21-ton coal hoppers. It is September 1970. These wagons were the mainstay of coal movements by rail from the 1950s though to the 1970s; the merry-go-round concept was still in the future. (John Glover)

As NCB No. 48 passes, the locomotive is seen in charge of ten 21-ton hopper wagons. Given that each wagon was 24 feet 6 inches long, the locomotive crew had to be aware of any obstructions 90 yards or so in front of them, and that applied whatever the weather, or if it was dark. The earlier coaling up of No. 48 seems to have managed to allocate some coal to the cab roof. (John Glover)

What became a substantial class of fifty-six locomotives, the British Railways Class 14 0-6-0 diesel hydraulics were built in 1964–65 at Swindon works. By April 1969, the whole lot had been withdrawn from BR service as surplus to requirements. They were sold to industry (forty-eight), or scrapped (eight). The National Coal Board acquired about one third of those sold; seen here is No. D9518. This became NCB No. 9312/95 when seen here at NCB Burradon in June 1970. (John Glover)

NCB No. 47 was an 0-6-0T built by Robert Stephenson & Hawthorn in 1955, works No. 7849. It is seen here with an internal user wagon at Backworth in June 1970. Short wheelbase steam locomotives were popular amongst industrial companies, since they were able to negotiate tight radius curves. Whether or not the wagons could also do so was another matter. (John Glover)

The NCB had numbers of often rather elderly wagons, which were confined to working within colliery premises and were not permitted to be used on British Rail tracks. To do so, they had to be certified as being of a condition up to the standard required. This one was seen at Burradon in their Northumberland area in June 1970, sporting a distinctive livery. (John Glover)

The last pit in Backworth, Eccles Colliery, was the deepest in Northumberland at 1,440 feet. It was 6 miles north-east of Newcastle. On 6 July 1972, Robert Stephenson & Hawthorn 0-6-0ST, works No. 7748 of 1953, NCB fleet No. 15, draws hoppers from the screens. The pit closed in July 1980. (David Young)

Robert Stephenson & Hawthorn 0-6-0ST (7097/43), also known as No. 9, is seen at Eccles Colliery, Backworth, on 10 June 1974. The pit employed 550 underground workers in 1947, plus another 180 on the surface – 730 in total. By the time of closure in 1980, this had reduced to a total of 526. (David Young)

It is Sunday 18 May 1967, so there is no activity on the staithes at North Blyth, which are full of wagons. Transfer of the coal from local collieries to coastal shipping for the onward journey was much used, with the railway only transporting that coal to the staithes. (John Glover)

Cumbria

The National Coal Board's Haig Colliery was perched high on the cliffs above Whitehaven, though its workings spread well under the Irish Sea. The colliery opened in 1916, closing eventually in 1986. Visiting it in June 1970, this Austerity 0-6-0ST was immediately noticeable from the dent in its water tank, the disfigured cab and a generally rather battered look from an earlier derailment. It did however sport a Giesl ejector. It is thought to have been built by Hudswell Clarke, works No. 1778 of 1944 – 'The Bent One'. (John Glover)

This is Haig Colliery, seen here on 13 June 1974, with Andrew Barclay 0-4-0ST No. 8 shunting some 21-ton hopper wagons. These were a standard British Railways design and the best part of 40,000 examples had been built by 1959, by BR and their LNER predecessor. (David Young)

Of a more modest size altogether were the NCB-owned wagons, seen here in June 1970. These comprised two main types: the side tippers (left) and the hoppers (right), which discharged through the bottom. It was important to match the wagon type with the unloading method to be used at their intended destination. (John Glover)

Andrew Barclay 0-4-0ST No. 8 is seen here at Ladysmith washery on 13 June 1974. Andrew Barclay of Kilmarnock were one of the most prolific builders of locomotives for the industrial market and their distinctive profile made identifying them relatively easy. (David Young)

21-ton hopper wagons are quite a handful, especially if, as here, they are to be hauled up (empties) or descend (loaded) an incline of this steepness. This is the Howgill Incline, linking the Haig Colliery and Ladysmith washery to the Whitehaven port area. The potential problem of buffer locking can be seen, as well as the very sudden gradient change. (John Glover)

The top of the Howgill Incline, in operation in June 1970. Inclines were commonplace in the early days of railways, for instance to haul trains from Euston for the first mile up Camden bank. However, as locomotives developed, they also became more powerful, so the need for external assistance reduced accordingly. Howgill was closed permanently in 1972. (John Glover)

The balancing working on the Howgill, with NCB internal use wagons, which used the incline in the course of carrying waste from the workings and depositing it in Whitehaven Harbour. The two 21-ton hoppers had suffered an earlier mishap and had yet to be removed. Who pays who for what in such circumstances? (John Glover)

Peckett 0-4-0ST (2028/42) *Victoria* has eight wagons from which quantities of colliery waste are to be discharged, and thus raising the level of the 'beach' below them just that bit more. Disposal of such items can be a major problem, but it is one that has to be managed by some means. Note the seat for the use of the operative during quiet periods. (John Glover)

The discharging of wagonloads of waste is not a pretty sight and it is a better reason to wear nose and mouth protection than many others. The variety of wagon types is quite surprising; one assumes that they have accumulated from a number of sources over many years. (John Glover)

This Robert Stephenson & Hawthorn 0-4-0ST (7049/42) is bringing some empty 21-ton hoppers along the side of the Whitehaven Docks to the bottom of the Howgill Incline. They will have come from the British Railways exchange sidings and will now be hauled up to Haig Colliery at the top and refilled. (John Glover)

Scotland

The line from Ayr to Dalmellington, which was to become part of the Glasgow & South Western Railway, was opened in 1856, but the passenger service south of Maybole Junction to the branch terminus closed on 6 April 1964. A private and steeply graded mineral branch was constructed from Waterside to collieries at Pennyvenie and Minnivey. This is Andrew Barclay 0-4-0ST, NCB No. 19 (1614/18), looking remarkably well cared for given its then age of fifty-eight years. (John Glover)

Andrew Barclay 0-6-0T No. 17 shunts spoil tippers at Minnivey, 22 November 1975. Built with works No. 1338 in 1913, the additional open wagon behind the cab was all but a fixture on this railway. It carried coal for the locomotive, in sufficient quantity that it would last at least until the next crew change. (David Young)

Level crossings can be a hazard for industrial railways too. This one, complete with a forbidding notice for road traffic, was just outside Minnivey. Here, the National Coal Board's No. 10 (AB 2244/47) is beginning to get underway, which means climbing over the hill and down to Waterside on 2 September 1969. (John Glover)

The National Coal Board's No. 10, with a payload of ten NCB-owned wagons, now has Minnivey well behind it and faces a steep climb on what might otherwise have been mistaken for a country branch line. It is en route for Dunaskin Washery, following which the coal will be loaded into British Railways wagons for onward transit. (John Glover)

This mixed train on the Waterside system consisted of four NCB side tipping wagons, Andrew Barclay locomotive No. 10 (2244/47), the ubiquitous coal tender, six British Railways 16-ton mineral wagons and ten National Coal Board internal user wagons. Quite what movement this entourage then made was not recorded. It was 2 September 1969. (John Glover)

Here, the empties are being returned to Pennyvenie behind Andrew Barclay No. 19 (AB 1614/18). The fireman in the coal wagon may be seen clearly, and he can now take it relatively easy as the hill has been climbed and the locomotive will be able to coast downhill to the Minnivey loop. It is 2 September 1969. Coal production ceased at Minnivey and Pennyvenie in 1978 and the railway serving them was closed. (John Glover)

This is the Whifflet foundry of R. B. Tennent Ltd at Coatbridge, Lanark. *Robin* is a product of the Sentinel company of Shrewsbury; it is a vertical boiler four-wheeled locomotive, works No. 9628 and dating from 1957. One of three then to be found on this site, it was photographed on 31 August 1970. (David Young)

R. Y. Pickering & Co.'s Wagon Works of Wishaw, Lanark, had their No. 4 in the works yard on 31 August 1970. This is a four-wheeled Sentinel vertical boiler locomotive, works No. 9559. It came to the Pickering company in 1968 from Rugby Portland Cement, Dunstable, to which it was delivered new in 1953. (David Young)

Near Glenboig, Bedlay Colliery was an important producer of coking coal for the iron and steel industry. The colliery's No. 6, an outside cylinder 0-4-0ST, brings its load to the weighbridge on 14 April 1981. Bedlay was opened in 1905 and was an important producer of coking coal for the iron and and steel industry. (David Young)

Bedlay Colliery's No. 8 starts away from the colliery on 11 September 1973. It does tend to give the impression of all smoke and little movement, but that will doubtless pass. The aim will be to take the wagons to the exchange sidings with British Railways on the former Monkland & Kirkintilloch branch. (David Young)

No. 17 is an 0-4-0ST from Andrew Barclay, works No. 2219 and built in 1946. It is seen here in Bedlay Colliery on 11 September 1973 in what can only be described as ex-works condition. It is, however, parked in a siding and the pit closed in 1981. (David Young)

Polkemmet was one of around eight collieries in the Whitburn area, roundly midway between Edinburgh and Glasgow, but most were closed by the 1960s. No. 15 was a rare survivor of a modest number of locomotives built by Grant Ritchie & Co. of Kilmarnock. This 0-4-2ST was works No. 539 and dated from 1917. It is seen here on 1 September 1969. (John Glover)

The National Coal Board's Polkemmet Colliery started production in 1921, employing a maximum of 2,000 or so at its peak output in 1960. It was the deepest pit in Scotland. Here, 0-6-0ST No. 25 (AB 2358/54) waits, while 0-6-0T No. 8 (AB 1296/15) has its coal supplies topped up, but not by using a shovel. It is 27 May 1977. (David Young)

On 1 September 1969, NCB Polkemmet No. 12, an Andrew Barclay 0-6-0ST (1829 of 1924), is taking its ease at the bottom of the incline before being required to head the wagons containing the colliery's recent output up to the exchange sidings with British Railways. (John Glover)

A remarkable sight at Polkemmet was the spectacle, usually, of two locomotives to take a train of loaded wagons up the hill to the exchange sidings with British Railways. Here, on 1 September 1969, Andrew Barclay 0-6-0ST (No. 1829 of 1924), No. 12, heads Hunslet 0-6-0ST (No. 2880 of 1943), No. 17, as they pound up the hill with much smoke and noise. One feels that this might not have been universally popular. (John Glover)

Polkemmet was a major supplier of coking coal for the steelworks at Ravenscraig. On 27 August 1970, No. 9 (AB 1235/11) heads uphill with a mere couple of wagons, while No. 8 (1175/09) returns light engine. But none of this is to be seen now; following severe flooding, which took place during the miners' strike, the colliery was closed in 1986. (David Young)

This is British Aluminium Co. (BAC), Burntisland, Fife. Bauxite, a key ingredient, was shipped to the docks, transferred to rail and brought to the works. These lay alongside the line between Aberdour and Kirkcaldy. Here, it was refined to recover the alumina, then transferred elsewhere for smelting to produce aluminium. The company's No. 1, a Peckett 0-4-0ST, works No. 1376 of 1915, is seen on 9 April 1971. (David Young)

At BAC's Burntisland works, opened in 1917, No. 3 shunts tank wagons on 9 April 1971. No. 3 is an Andrew Barclay 0-4-0ST, works No. 2046 of 1937. Roughly 4 tons of dried bauxite produces 2 tons of alumina, which in turn produces 1 ton of aluminium. In 1972 the plant switched to producing special chemicals and in 1982 the company was acquired by Alcan. (David Young)

The Peckett 0-4-0ST No. 1 of the British Aluminium Co. at Burntisland propels three 16-ton mineral wagons to the back of the works area on 9 April 1971. After eighty-five years of operation, the plant was closed in 2002, the site was levelled and it has now been transformed into a housing estate. (David Young)

National Coal Board 0-4-0ST No. 47 (AB2157/43) gives rear end assistance to a British Rail coal train out of Kinneil Colliery yard on 28 August 1970. This section is now part of the Bo'ness & Kinneil Railway, operated by the Scottish Railway Preservation Society. Kinneil was to be 'a major colliery in the great reconstruction programme', which ran from 1951 to 1956. It closed on 14 December 1982, the NCB citing geological difficulties. (David Young)

Comrie Colliery opened in 1939, with men reaching the coal face, 1,200 feet down, in a cage taking two minutes. A separate shaft was used for coal extraction. When it reached the surface it was screened, picked over, washed, sized and graded. This is the railway yard with the 0-6-0ST Austerity No. 19 on 10 September 1973. (David Young)

No. 19 was built for the National Coal Board by Hunslet in 1954. In its by now bright livery of primary colours, the locomotive is seen returning from Oakley yard to Comrie Colliery with empties on 17 April 1981. The colliery could achieve an output of 400 tons of coal per hour. In 1983, three-quarters of that was going to the South of Scotland Electricity Board. (David Young)

On 12 April 1971, Comrie Colliery's No. 7, a William Bagnall-built 0-6-0ST, works No. 2777 of 1945, brings empties into the National Coal Board's yard. Comrie was billed as a model colliery, its keynotes being 'safety, efficiency and economy'. But that didn't last, and Comrie closed in 1986, in common with so many others. (David Young)

The National Coal Board's No. 6 was an 0-4-0ST built by Andrew Barclay in 1949, works No. 2261. It is seen here carrying out shunting at Blairhall Colliery, Fife. The colliery was opened in the 1880s, and by 1948 around 1,200 tons of coal and ironstone were being produced daily. It was served by a branch off the Stirling to Dunfermline railway. The colliery was closed permanently in 1969. (David Young)

The Wemyss Private Railway was a network of mineral lines on private land in Fife, connecting coal pits to harbours and to the national railway system. It included Wellesley Colliery. This is their No. 14 Hunslet 0-6-0ST, works No. 2888 of 1943. It is 31 August 1969 and falling traffic levels meant that the railway would close in the following year. (John Glover)

On the left is the hefty-looking Wemyss Private Railway No. 20, an Andrew Barclay 0-6-0T, works No. 2068 of 1939. On the right is NCB No. 8, Andrew Barclay 0-6-0ST, works No. 1175 of 1909. They are seen together in Methil yard, Dysart, on 27 March 1970. (David Young)

Wemyss Private Railway No. 17 was one of those massive 0-6-0T locomotives built for them by Andrew Barclay of Kilmarnock in 1935, works No. 2017. It is 27 March 1970. These successful locomotives eventually totalled five; they had a tractive effort of 22,403 lb, or almost as the much as the 'Austerity' tanks of some years later. (David Young)

The Wemyss Private Railway's second No. 16 was an 'Austerity' 0-6-0ST, built by William Bagnall as works No. 2759 in 1944. This did not become part of the WPR fleet until 1964 and is seen here in Methil yard on 27 March 1970. The Wemyss fleet eventually included five of these locomotives. Methil docks were once the largest coal exporting port in Scotland. (David Young)

And Finally

This Andrew Barclay 0-4-0ST (1608/18) *Blaenavon Lily No 8* was photographed at Celynon South Colliery in the South Wales Valleys on 4 January 1969. It looked very much as being past its best before date, and towards the end of its career with the National Coal Board. Sadly, such an appearance was not uncommon in the latter days of steam working. (John Glover)

Given the willpower, sheer hard work and some funding, locomotives can be restored. This is Andrew Barclay 0-4-0ST *The Blaenavon Co Ltd NORA No 5*, works No. 1680 and built in 1920. It is on display outside the Big Pit National Coal Museum in Wales, opened in 1983. It is 23 May 2010. (John Glover)